Disclaimer

First printing edition 2024.
Publisher: James Benedict

Paperback ISBN: 978-1-955419-14-7
ebook ISBN: 978-1-955419-15-4
Publisher   :   James Benedict
Language   :   English
Paperback   :   142 pages
Dimensions   :   28x 21.6 cm

MRP: $29.99

AFRICAN ELEPHANT

● **Habitat:** Kenya, South Africa; found in savannas and grasslands.

● **Lifespan:** Up to 60–70 years.

● **Diet:** Herbivore; feeds on grasses and foliage.

● **Behavior:** Social animals living in herds led by females.

● **Threats:** Endangered due to poaching and habitat loss.

ALLIGATOR

● **Habitat:** Found in the United States; resides in freshwater habitats.
● **Lifespan:** Around 35–50 years.
● **Diet:** Carnivore; preys on fish, birds, and mammals.
● **Behavior:** Cold-blooded reptiles known for lurking in water bodies.
● **Conservation Status:** Considered of Least Concern.

ARMADILLOS

- **Habitat:** Found in Argentina; lives in grasslands and forests.
- **Lifespan:** Around 4-5 years in the wild.
- **Diet:** Omnivore; feeds on insects, small vertebrates, and plants.
- **Behavior:** Armored mammals known for rolling into a ball for protection.
- **Conservation Status:** Various species face threats due to habitat loss and hunting.

ALBATROSS

● **Habitat:** Various coastal regions globally.

● **Lifespan:** Up to 50 years or more.

● **Diet:** Carnivore; scavenges on fish, squid, and krill.

● **Behavior:** Exceptional gliding birds covering vast distances over oceans.

● **Conservation Status:** Several species face threats like bycatch and habitat degradation.

ANACONDA

- **Habitat:** Found in South America; primarily inhabits freshwater habitats.
- **Lifespan:** Estimated up to 10–12 years in the wild.
- **Diet:** Carnivore; preys on aquatic animals like fish and mammals.
- **Behavior:** Large constrictor snakes, ambush predators.
- **Conservation Status:** Generally not evaluated, but some species face threats.

ANGELFISH

- **Habitat:** Found in various tropical oceans.
- **Lifespan:** Varies among species, generally 5-15 years.
- **Diet:** Omnivore; feeds on algae, small invertebrates, and plankton.
- **Behavior:** Colorful reef fish known for their distinctive shapes.
- **Conservation Status:** Various species face threats due to habitat degradation and overfishing.

AARDVARK

- **Habitat:** Inhabit savannas and grasslands across Africa.
- **Lifespan:** Typically 10–15 years in the wild.
- **Diet:** Insectivore; primarily feeds on ants and termites.
- **Behavior:** Nocturnal animals with long ears and tubular snouts.
- **Conservation Status:** Generally not threatened, but some populations face habitat loss.

BALD EAGLE

- **Habitat:** United States; resides near lakes, rivers, and coasts.
- **Lifespan:** Around 20-30 years.
- **Diet:** Carnivore; mainly feeds on fish and waterfowl.
- **Behavior:** Majestic birds known for their impressive hunting skills.
- **Conservation Status:** Recovered from endangered status but still protected.

BLUE WHALE

● **Habitat:** Found in various oceans globally.

● **Lifespan:** Estimated to be around 70-90 years.

● **Diet:** Filter feeder; primarily consumes krill and small fish.

● **Behavior:** Largest animals on Earth; undertake long migrations.

● **Conservation Status:** Endangered due to historical hunting practices.

BEAVER

- **Habitat:** Canada; primarily found in freshwater habitats.
- **Lifespan:** Typically 10–15 years in the wild.
- **Diet:** Herbivore; feeds on bark, leaves, and aquatic plants.
- **Behavior:** Semi-aquatic mammals known for building dams and lodges.
- **Conservation Status:** Considered of Least Concern.

BENGAL TIGER

● **Habitat:** India; resides in forests and grasslands.

● **Lifespan:** Around 10–15 years in the wild.

● **Diet:** Carnivore; hunts deer, wild boars, and other large mammals.

● **Behavior:** Solitary hunters with remarkable strength and agility.

● **Conservation Status:** Endangered due to poaching and habitat loss.

BISON

- **Habitat:** United States; roams in grasslands and plains.
- **Lifespan:** Generally 15–20 years in the wild.
- **Diet:** Herbivore; grazes on grasses and sedges.
- **Behavior:** Massive mammals with a social structure in herds.
- **Conservation Status:** Near-threatened due to historical population decline.

BLUEFIN TUNA

● **Habitat:** Found globally in various oceans.

● **Lifespan:** Up to 15–30 years.

● **Diet:** Carnivore; preys on smaller fish and squid.

● **Behavior:** Highly migratory fish, important for commercial fishing.

● **Conservation Status:** Threatened due to overfishing and high market demand.

BOA CONSTRICTOR

- **Habitat:** South America; inhabits various forested habitats.
- **Lifespan:** Typically 20-30 years in the wild.
- **Diet:** Carnivore; ambushes and constricts prey, primarily small mammals and birds.
- **Behavior:** Large constrictor snakes known for their muscular bodies.
- **Conservation Status:** Generally not evaluated, but some species may face threats

BARRACUDA

- Habitat: Found in warm oceans.
- Lifespan: Typically 10-15 years.
- Diet: Carnivore; preys on smaller fish, including reef fish.
- Behavior: Fast-swimming predatory fish with elongated bodies.
- Conservation Status: Generally not evaluated; populations can face overfishing.

BABOON

● **Habitat:** Africa; inhabits savannas and woodlands.

● **Lifespan:** Around 20–30 years in the wild.

● **Diet:** Omnivore; feeds on fruits, seeds, and occasionally small animals.

● **Behavior:** Social primates living in troops with complex social structures.

● **Conservation Status:** Generally not threatened, but some populations face habitat loss and hunting pressure.

CROCODILE

- **Habitat:** Egypt; primarily resides in freshwater habitats.
- **Lifespan:** Typically 70–100 years.
- **Diet:** Carnivore; preys on fish, birds, and mammals.
- **Behavior:** Large reptiles with powerful jaws, known for ambush hunting.
- **Conservation Status:** Generally not evaluated; some populations may face threats.

CAPYBARA

● **Habitat:** Found in Argentina; resides in grasslands and wetlands.

● **Lifespan:** Typically 8–10 years in the wild.

● **Diet:** Herbivore; grazes on grasses and aquatic plants.

● **Behavior:** Largest rodents, often seen in groups near water.

● **Conservation Status:** Generally not threatened; abundant in some regions.

CARIBOU

● **Habitat:** Canada; migratory herds found in tundra and boreal forests.

● **Lifespan:** Around 10–15 years in the wild.

● **Diet:** Herbivore; grazes on lichens, grasses, and shrubs.

● **Behavior:** Migratory mammals, known for their large antlers.

● **Conservation Status:** Various subspecies face threats due to habitat degradation and climate change.

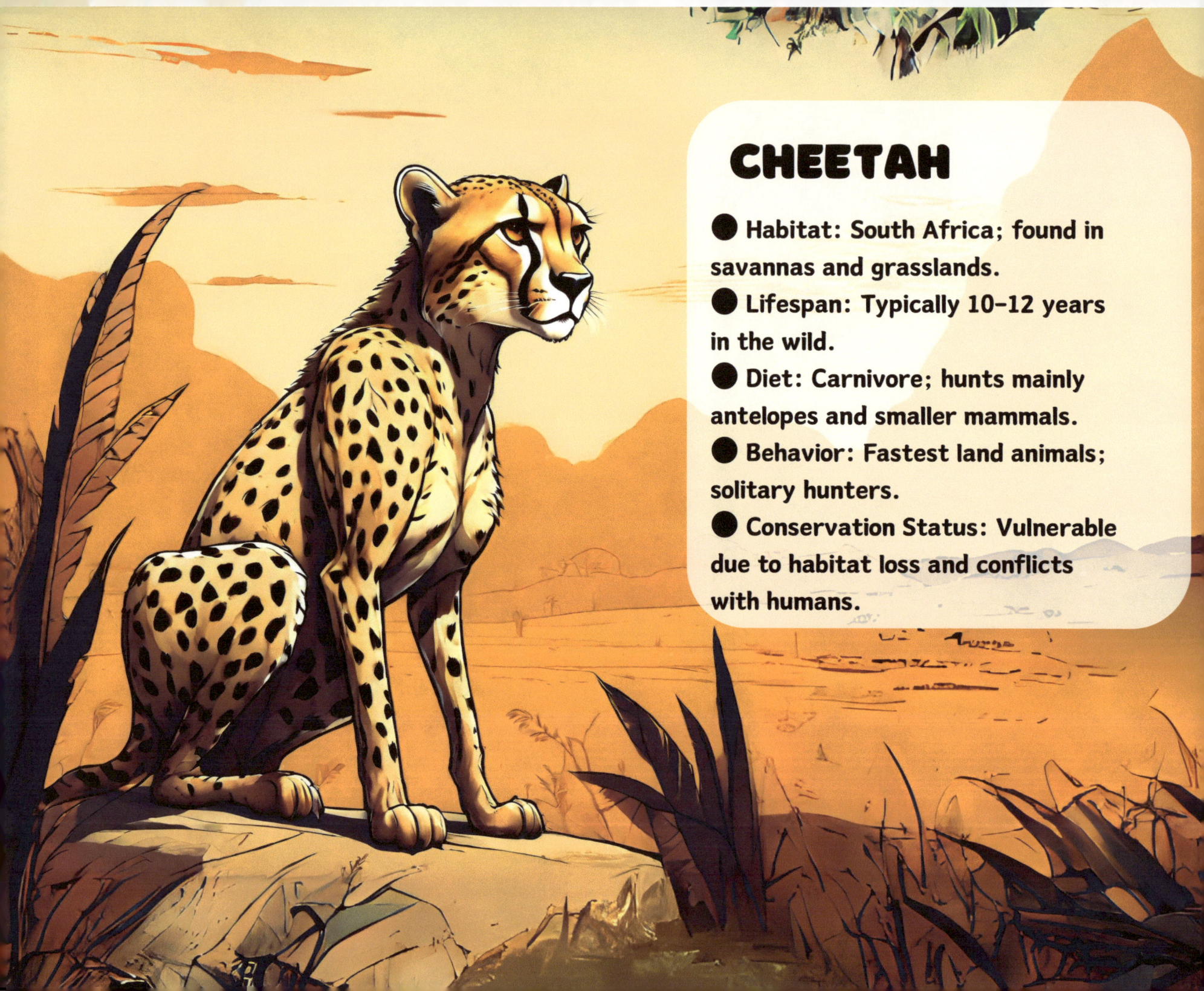

CHEETAH

● **Habitat:** South Africa; found in savannas and grasslands.
● **Lifespan:** Typically 10–12 years in the wild.
● **Diet:** Carnivore; hunts mainly antelopes and smaller mammals.
● **Behavior:** Fastest land animals; solitary hunters.
● **Conservation Status:** Vulnerable due to habitat loss and conflicts with humans.

COATI

- **Habitat:** Found in Mexico; inhabits forests and woodlands.
- **Lifespan:** Around 7–8 years in the wild.
- **Diet:** Omnivore; feeds on insects, fruits, and small vertebrates.
- **Behavior:** Social animals living in groups called bands.
- **Conservation Status:** Generally not evaluated; populations may face habitat loss.

CHIMPANZEE

● **Habitat:** Found in various countries in Africa.

● **Lifespan:** Around 40–50 years in the wild.

● **Diet:** Omnivore; feeds on fruits, nuts, and occasionally insects.

● **Behavior:** Highly intelligent primates, live in communities.

● **Conservation Status:** Endangered due to habitat loss and hunting.

CONDOR

● **Habitat:** Various species found in South America.

● **Lifespan:** Can live up to 50–60 years.

● **Diet:** Carnivore; scavenges on carrion.

● **Behavior:** Large vultures with impressive wingspans.

● **Conservation Status:** Threatened due to habitat loss and accidental poisoning.

CLOWNFISH

- **Habitat:** Found in coral reefs of the Pacific and Indian Oceans.
- **Lifespan:** Around 6-10 years.
- **Diet:** Omnivore; feeds on algae and small invertebrates.
- **Behavior:** Colorful reef fish often associated with sea anemones.
- **Conservation Status:** Generally not evaluated; some populations face threats from habitat degradation and collection for the aquarium trade.

DEER

● **Habitat:** Various species found in the United Kingdom.

● **Lifespan:** Varies by species, typically 4–8 years.

● **Diet:** Herbivore; feeds on grasses, leaves, and shrubs.

● **Behavior:** Social animals, often seen in small groups.

● **Conservation Status:** Various species face threats due to habitat loss and hunting pressure.

DOLPHIN

● **Habitat:** Various species found in oceans worldwide.

● **Lifespan:** Ranges from 20-50 years.

● **Diet:** Carnivore; feeds on fish, squid, and crustaceans.

● **Behavior:** Highly intelligent and social marine mammals.

● **Conservation Status:** Some species are threatened due to bycatch, habitat degradation, and pollution.

DINGO

- **Habitat:** Found in Australia; lives in diverse habitats.
- **Lifespan:** Typically 10–15 years in the wild.
- **Diet:** Carnivore; hunts small mammals and scavenges.
- **Behavior:** Wild dogs, often considered a native species of Australia.
- **Conservation Status:** Not threatened; considered a cultural icon in Australia

ABC
ANIMALS

E

ELEPHANT SEAL

● **Habitat:** Found in various coastal regions, especially around Antarctica.

● **Lifespan:** Around 20-22 years.

● **Diet:** Carnivore; feeds on fish and squid.

● **Behavior:** Large seals known for their size and fighting among males.

● **Conservation Status:** Generally not evaluated; some populations may face threats.

ELEPHANT (INDIA)

- **Habitat:** Indian Elephants in forests.
- **Lifespan:** Up to 60-70 years.
- **Diet:** Herbivore; feeds on grasses, leaves, and fruits.
- **Behavior:** Social animals, living in herds led by matriarchs.
- **Conservation Status:** African Elephants are endangered, while Indian Elephants are vulnerable due to habitat loss and poaching.

EMU

● **Habitat:** Found in Australia; inhabits savannas and woodlands.

● **Lifespan:** Typically 10–20 years.

● **Diet:** Omnivore; feeds on fruits, seeds, and insects.

● **Behavior:** Flightless birds known for their speed and large size.

● **Conservation Status:** Not threatened; considered a national symbol in Australia.

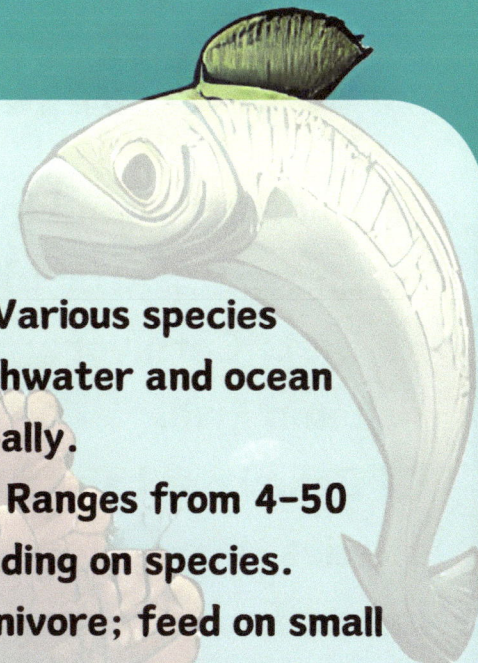

EEL

● **Habitat:** Various species found in freshwater and ocean habitats globally.

● **Lifespan:** Ranges from 4-50 years, depending on species.

● **Diet:** Carnivore; feed on small fish, invertebrates, and sometimes plants.

● **Behavior:** Long, snake-like fish known for their slimy appearance.

● **Conservation Status:** Some species are threatened due to habitat degradation and overfishing.

EMPEROR PENGUIN

- Habitat: Found in Antarctica.
- Lifespan: Around 20 years.
- Diet: Carnivore; mainly eats fish and krill.
- Behavior: Largest penguin species, known for their breeding habits and parenting.
- Conservation Status: Vulnerable due to climate change affecting sea ice.

F

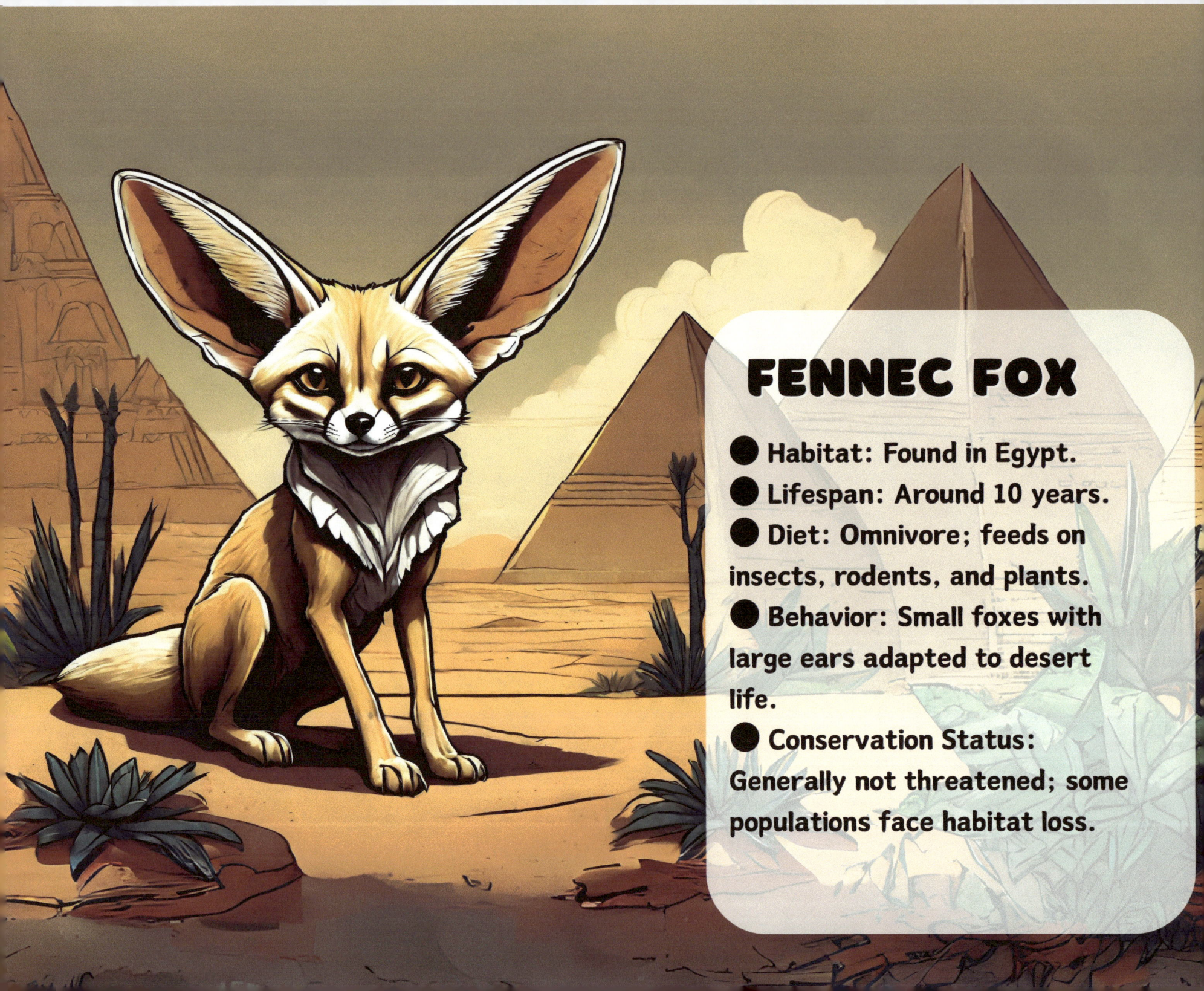

FENNEC FOX

- **Habitat:** Found in Egypt.
- **Lifespan:** Around 10 years.
- **Diet:** Omnivore; feeds on insects, rodents, and plants.
- **Behavior:** Small foxes with large ears adapted to desert life.
- **Conservation Status:** Generally not threatened; some populations face habitat loss.

FLAMINGO

● **Habitat:** Various species found in different regions worldwide.

● **Lifespan:** Around 40-60 years.

● **Diet:** Omnivore; feeds on algae, crustaceans, and small fish.

● **Behavior:** Colorful wading birds known for their distinctive long legs and necks.

● **Conservation Status:** Some species are threatened due to habitat loss and pollution.

FLYING FISH

● **Habitat:** Found in various oceans.
● **Lifespan:** Up to 5 years.
● **Diet:** Carnivore; feeds on plankton and small fish.
● **Behavior:** Known for their unique ability to glide above the water's surface.
● **Conservation Status:** Not threatened; abundant in many oceanic regions.

GIANT PANDA

- **Habitat:** Found in China.
- **Lifespan:** Around 20 years in the wild.
- **Diet:** Herbivore; almost entirely feeds on bamboo.
- **Behavior:** Solitary except during mating season; iconic black and white bears.
- **Conservation Status:** Endangered due to habitat loss and low reproduction rates.

GIRAFFE

- **Habitat:** Found in Kenya.
- **Lifespan:** Around 25 years in the wild.
- **Diet:** Herbivore; feeds on leaves from tall trees.
- **Behavior:** Tallest land animals with distinctive long necks and spotted coats.
- **Conservation Status:** Vulnerable due to habitat loss and illegal hunting.

GOLDEN MONKEY

- **Habitat:** Found in China.
- **Lifespan:** Around 15–20 years in the wild.
- **Diet:** Primarily herbivores; feed on leaves, fruits, and insects.
- **Behavior:** Sociable primates living in groups.
- **Conservation Status:** Endangered due to habitat loss and poaching.

GRIZZLY BEAR

- **Habitat:** Found in the United States.
- **Lifespan:** Typically 20–25 years.
- **Diet:** Omnivore; feeds on fish, berries, and small mammals.
- **Behavior:** Large and powerful bears, excellent swimmers and climbers.
- **Conservation Status:** Generally not threatened, but some populations face habitat loss.

GORILLA

- **Habitat:** Found in Africa.
- **Lifespan:** Around 35–40 years in the wild.
- **Diet:** Primarily herbivores; consume leaves, fruits, and some insects.
- **Behavior:** Largest primates, live in cohesive groups.
- **Conservation Status:** Endangered due to habitat loss, poaching, and diseases.

GROUSE

● **Habitat:** Various species found in different regions worldwide.

● **Lifespan:** Ranges from 1-10 years, depending on species.

● **Diet:** Herbivore; feeds on plants, seeds, and insects.

● **Behavior:** Ground-dwelling birds known for their elaborate courtship displays.

● **Conservation Status:** Some species face threats due to habitat loss and hunting.

GANNET

● **Habitat:** Various species found in different regions worldwide.

● **Lifespan:** Around 15-25 years.

● **Diet:** Carnivore; feeds on fish by plunge diving.

● **Behavior:** Seabirds with exceptional diving abilities.

● **Conservation Status:** Some populations are vulnerable due to fishing pressures and pollution.

ABC ANIMALS

H

HORSE

● Habitat: Global, in various climates.

● Lifespan: About 25-30 years.

● Diet: Herbivore, eating grass and grains.

● Behavior: Social animals known for strength and adaptability.

● Conservation Status: Wild populations at risk due to habitat loss.

HEDGEHOG

- **Habitat: Found in the United Kingdom.**
- **Lifespan: Around 2-5 years in the wild.**
- **Diet: Omnivore; feeds on insects, worms, and fruits.**
- **Behavior: Nocturnal mammals with spines for defense.**
- **Conservation Status: Generally not threatened; some populations may face habitat loss.**

HUMPBACK WHALE

● **Habitat:** Found in various oceans globally.
● **Lifespan:** Around 50 years.
● **Diet:** Filter feeder; mainly consumes krill and small fish.
● **Behavior:** Known for acrobatic behavior such as breaching and slapping the water with fins.
● **Conservation Status:** Vulnerable due to historical hunting but populations are recovering.

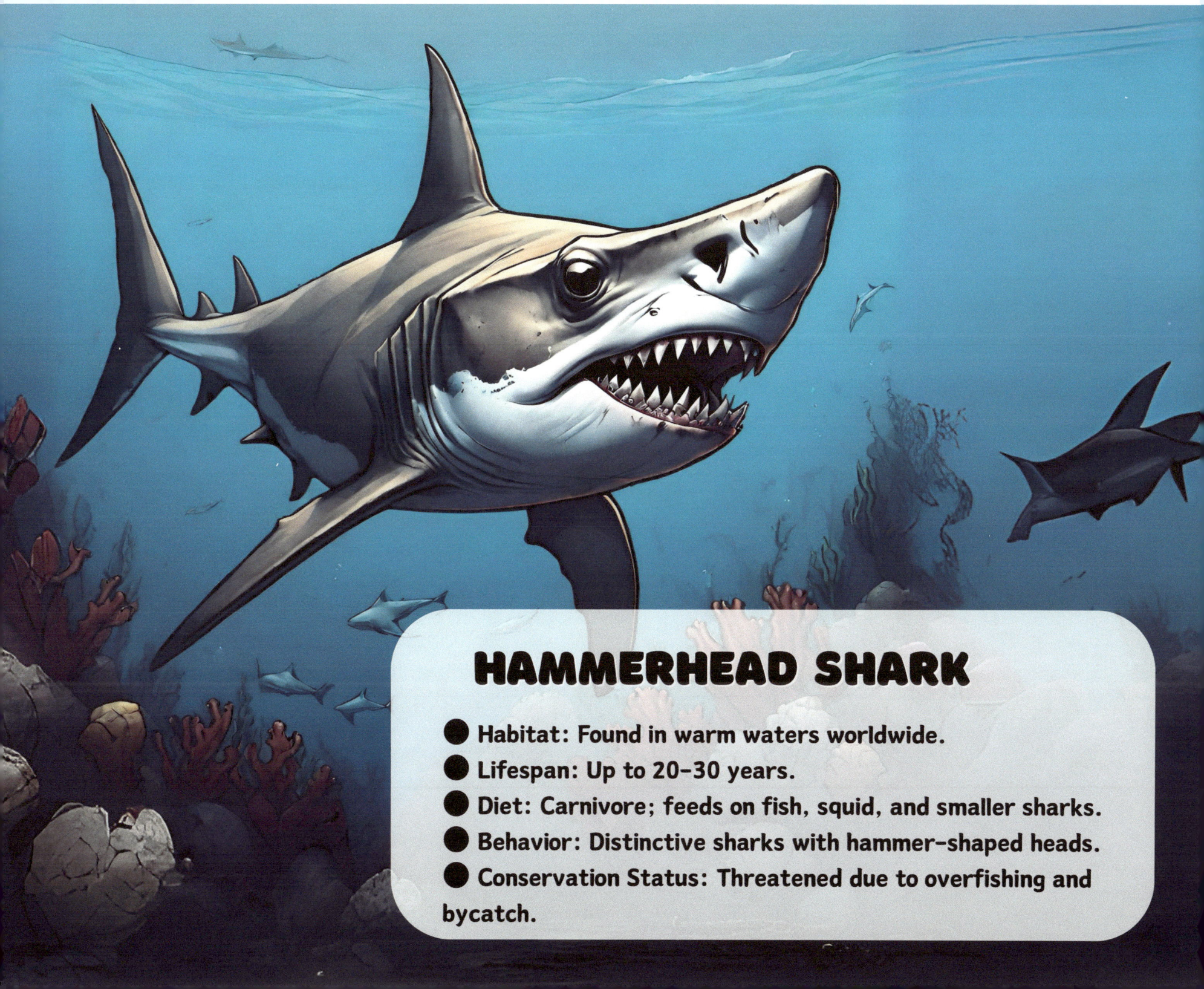

HAMMERHEAD SHARK

- **Habitat:** Found in warm waters worldwide.
- **Lifespan:** Up to 20–30 years.
- **Diet:** Carnivore; feeds on fish, squid, and smaller sharks.
- **Behavior:** Distinctive sharks with hammer-shaped heads.
- **Conservation Status:** Threatened due to overfishing and bycatch.

IBEX

- Habitat: Found in France.
- Lifespan: Typically around 10-15 years.
- Diet: Herbivore; feeds on grasses, herbs, and shrubs.
- Behavior: Wild goats adapted to rugged mountainous terrain.
- Conservation Status: Generally not threatened; protected in many regions.

INDIAN RHINOCEROS

- **Habitat:** Found in India.
- **Lifespan:** Around 35–40 years.
- **Diet:** Herbivore; primarily grazes on grasses and leaves.
- **Behavior:** Large herbivores with a single horn.
- **Conservation Status:** Vulnerable due to poaching and habitat loss.

J

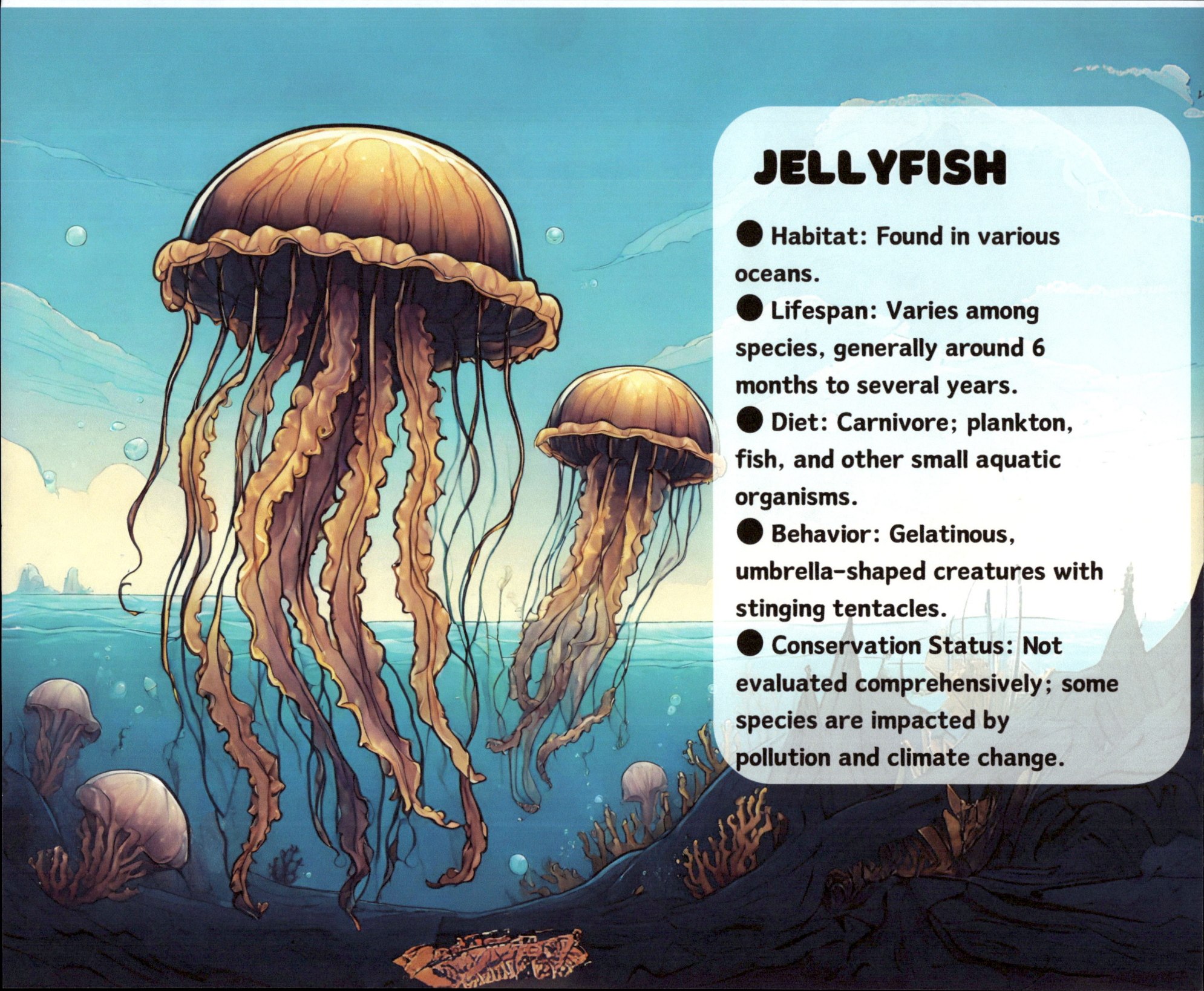

JELLYFISH

● **Habitat:** Found in various oceans.

● **Lifespan:** Varies among species, generally around 6 months to several years.

● **Diet:** Carnivore; plankton, fish, and other small aquatic organisms.

● **Behavior:** Gelatinous, umbrella-shaped creatures with stinging tentacles.

● **Conservation Status:** Not evaluated comprehensively; some species are impacted by pollution and climate change.

JAGUAR

- **Habitat:** Found in Brazil and Mexico.
- **Lifespan:** Typically around 12–15 years in the wild.
- **Diet:** Carnivore; hunts various mammals and reptiles.
- **Behavior:** Powerful and elusive big cats; proficient swimmers.
- **Conservation Status:** Near-threatened due to habitat loss and conflicts with humans.

JAPANESE MACAQUE

- **Habitat:** Found in Japan.
- **Lifespan:** Around 20-30 years in the wild.
- **Diet:** Omnivore; feeds on fruits, leaves, and small animals.
- **Behavior:** Highly social monkeys known for their adaptations to cold climates.
- **Conservation Status:** Not threatened; adaptations help them survive in varied habitats.

JAY

● **Habitat:** Various species found in different regions worldwide.

● **Lifespan:** Typically around 5-7 years.

● **Diet:** Omnivore; feeds on seeds, insects, and small vertebrates.

● **Behavior:** Medium-sized birds known for their raucous calls.

● **Conservation Status:** Generally not evaluated; populations may face habitat loss.

K

KANGAROO

- **Habitat:** Found in Australia.
- **Lifespan:** Ranges from 6-20 years, depending on species.
- **Diet:** Herbivore; grazes on grasses and plants.
- **Behavior:** Marsupials known for hopping and carrying young in pouches.
- **Conservation Status:** Various species face threats due to habitat loss and hunting.

KEA

● **Habitat:** Found in New Zealand.

● **Lifespan:** Around 5-10 years in the wild.

● **Diet:** Omnivore; feeds on fruits, seeds, and insects.

● **Behavior:** Intelligent parrots known for their curiosity and problem-solving skills.

● **Conservation Status:** Vulnerable due to habitat loss and interactions with humans.

KIWI

● Habitat: Found in New Zealand.

● Lifespan: Typically 20–30 years.

● Diet: Omnivore; feeds on invertebrates, fruits, and seeds.

● Behavior: Flightless birds with long bills and nocturnal habits.

● Conservation Status: Endangered due to habitat loss and predators.

KOALA

- **Habitat:** Found in Australia.
- **Lifespan:** Around 10–15 years in the wild.
- **Diet:** Herbivore; feeds almost exclusively on eucalyptus leaves.
- **Behavior:** Arboreal marsupials known for sleeping long hours.
- **Conservation Status:** Vulnerable due to habitat loss and diseases.

KINGFISHER

● **Habitat:** Various species found in different regions worldwide.

● **Lifespan:** Typically 6–10 years.

● **Diet:** Carnivore; feeds on fish and aquatic insects.

● **Behavior:** Colorful birds with rapid dives into water for prey.

● **Conservation Status:** Generally not threatened; some species face habitat loss.

KILLER WHALE (ORCA)

- Habitat: Found in various oceans.
- Lifespan: Up to 50–80 years.
- Diet: Apex predators feeding on fish, seals, and other marine mammals.
- Behavior: Highly social marine mammals known for their hunting strategies.
- Conservation Status: Not threatened; adaptable and widespread.

KRILL

- **Habitat:** Found in various oceans, forming a critical part of the marine food web.
- **Lifespan:** Typically up to 6 years.
- **Diet:** Filter-feeders; consume phytoplankton and small zooplankton.
- **Behavior:** Small crustaceans forming massive swarms.
- **Conservation Status:** Not evaluated; vital prey for numerous marine species.

LION

- Habitat: Found in Kenya, South Africa, and other African regions.
- Lifespan: Typically 10–14 years in the wild.
- Diet: Carnivore; hunts various large mammals in prides.
- Behavior: Social cats living in groups known as prides.
- Conservation Status: Vulnerable due to habitat loss and conflicts with humans.

LEOPARD

- **Habitat:** Sub-Saharan Africa, parts of Asia; forests, grasslands.
- **Lifespan:** 12–17 years in the wild.
- **Diet:** Carnivore, hunting various mammals.
- **Behavior:** Solitary, skilled climbers and hunters.
- **Conservation Status:** Near-threatened due to poaching and habitat loss.

LYNX

- **Habitat:** Found in Germany and other European regions.
- **Lifespan:** Around 10-15 years in the wild.
- **Diet:** Carnivore; primarily hunts smaller mammals.
- **Behavior:** Solitary and elusive cats with tufted ears.
- **Conservation Status:** Some populations are threatened due to habitat loss and hunting.

LEMUR

● Habitat: Found in Madagascar.

● Lifespan: Around 15-20 years in the wild.

● Diet: Primarily herbivores; feed on fruits, leaves, and insects.

● Behavior: Arboreal primates with diverse species and social structures.

● Conservation Status: Endangered due to habitat loss and illegal pet trade.

LOBSTER

- **Habitat:** Found in oceans worldwide, primarily in rocky or sandy areas.
- **Lifespan:** Varies; some can live for over 50 years.
- **Diet:** Omnivore; scavengers feeding on dead fish, algae, and small invertebrates.
- **Behavior:** Crustaceans with hard exoskeletons and prominent claws.
- **Conservation Status:** Generally not evaluated; some populations face overfishing.

LEATHERBACK TURTLE

● **Habitat:** Found in tropical oceans worldwide.
● **Lifespan:** Around 30-45 years.
● **Diet:** Carnivore; primarily eats jellyfish.
● **Behavior:** Largest sea turtles known for their leathery shells.
● **Conservation Status:** Vulnerable due to fishing gear entanglement and habitat loss.

MONKEY

- **Habitat:** Across Africa, Asia, Americas; varied regions.
- **Lifespan:** Varies, some up to 20-30 years.
- **Diet:** Omnivore, consuming fruits, insects, and small animals.
- **Behavior:** Social animals with complex communication.
- **Conservation Status:** Various species endangered due to habitat destruction.

MOOSE

- **Habitat:** Found in Canada.
- **Lifespan:** Typically 15–25 years.
- **Diet:** Herbivore; primarily feeds on aquatic plants and twigs.
- **Behavior:** Largest deer species with distinctive palmate antlers.
- **Conservation Status:** Generally not threatened; managed hunting practices in some regions.

MANATEE

● Habitat: Found in various coastal regions, especially in warm waters.

● Lifespan: Around 40 years.

● Diet: Herbivore; feeds on aquatic plants and grasses.

● Behavior: Large, slow-moving marine mammals known for their gentle nature.

● Conservation Status: Vulnerable due to habitat loss and collisions with boats.

MANTA RAY

● **Habitat:** Found in various oceans.

● **Lifespan:** Around 20-30 years.

● **Diet:** Filter-feeders; primarily consume plankton and small fish.

● **Behavior:** Large rays with distinctive wing-like pectoral fins.

● **Conservation Status:** Vulnerable due to bycatch and habitat degradation.

MEERKAT

- **Habitat:** Found in Africa.
- **Lifespan:** Around 12–14 years in the wild.
- **Diet:** Omnivore; feeds on insects, small mammals, and plants.
- **Behavior:** Highly social animals living in groups called mobs or gangs.
- **Conservation Status:** Not threatened; widespread in suitable habitats.

MONGOOSE

- **Habitat:** Various species found in different regions worldwide.
- **Lifespan:** Ranges from 6–13 years.
- **Diet:** Omnivore; feeds on insects, small rodents, and fruits.
- **Behavior:** Agile and opportunistic hunters.
- **Conservation Status:** Generally not threatened; adaptable to various environments.

MONARCH BUTTERFLY

● **Habitat:** Found in various continents during migrations.

● **Lifespan:** Typically 6-8 months (migratory generations).

● **Diet:** Herbivore; feeds on nectar from flowers as adults.

● **Behavior:** Known for their incredible long-distance migrations.

● **Conservation Status:** Not threatened; population fluctuations due to habitat loss.

MOUNTAIN GOAT

- **Habitat:** Found in various mountainous regions.
- **Lifespan:** Around 12–15 years in the wild.
- **Diet:** Herbivore; grazes on grasses, herbs, and shrubs.
- **Behavior:** Sure-footed climbers adapted to rocky terrains.
- **Conservation Status:** Not threatened; managed populations in some regions.

MAGPIE

- **Habitat:** Various species found in different regions worldwide.
- **Lifespan:** Typically 3–4 years.
- **Diet:** Omnivore; feeds on insects, seeds, and small animals.
- **Behavior:** Known for their striking black and white plumage.
- **Conservation Status:** Generally not threatened; adaptable and widespread.

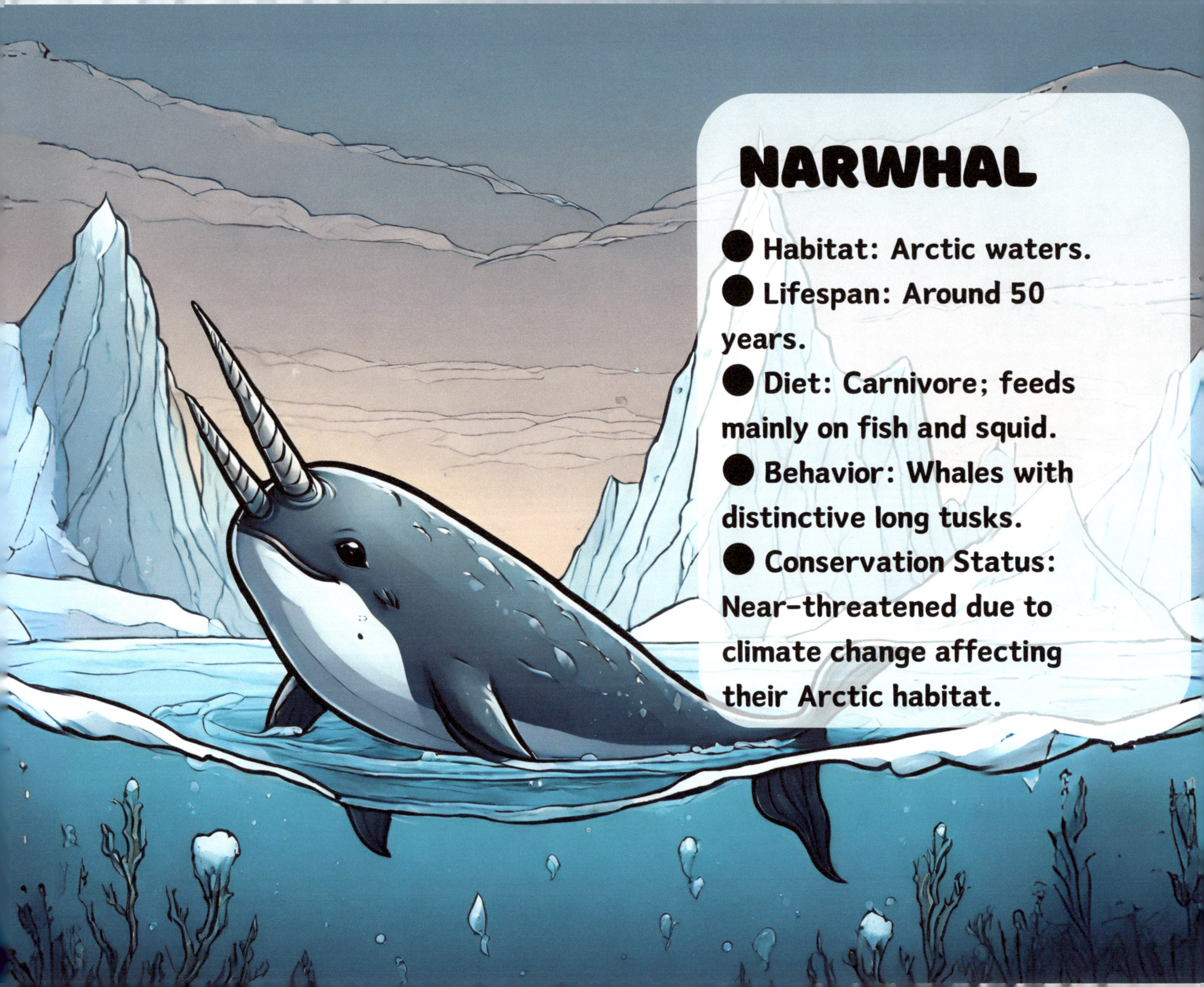

NARWHAL

- **Habitat:** Arctic waters.
- **Lifespan:** Around 50 years.
- **Diet:** Carnivore; feeds mainly on fish and squid.
- **Behavior:** Whales with distinctive long tusks.
- **Conservation Status:** Near-threatened due to climate change affecting their Arctic habitat.

NIGHTINGALE

● Habitat: Found in Europe, Asia, and Africa in woodland habitats.

● Lifespan: Around 2-3 years.

● Diet: Insectivore; feeds on insects and spiders.

● Behavior: Singing birds known for melodious and complex songs.

● Conservation Status: Generally stable, but some populations face habitat loss.

OSTRICH

- **Habitat:** Found in Africa.
- **Lifespan:** Typically around 30-40 years.
- **Diet:** Omnivore; mainly consumes plants and occasionally insects.
- **Behavior:** Largest and fastest birds, incapable of flight.
- **Conservation Status:** Not threatened; farmed in various regions.

OCTOPUS

- **Habitat:** Found in oceans worldwide.
- **Lifespan:** Varies by species, typically 1-2 years.
- **Diet:** Carnivore; preys on crustaceans, mollusks, and fish.
- **Behavior:** Intelligent invertebrates with complex behaviors and camouflage abilities.
- **Conservation Status:** Not evaluated; some species may face threats from overfishing.

OTTER

- **Habitat:** Various species found in different regions worldwide.
- **Lifespan:** Ranges from 10–15 years.
- **Diet:** Carnivore; feeds on fish, crustaceans, and amphibians.
- **Behavior:** Aquatic mammals known for playful behavior.
- **Conservation Status:** Some populations threatened due to habitat loss and pollution.

ORANGUTAN

● **Habitat:** Found in Indonesia and Malaysia.

● **Lifespan:** Around 30-45 years in the wild.

● **Diet:** Primarily herbivores; consume fruits, leaves, and insects.

● **Behavior:** Highly intelligent primates, mostly arboreal.

● **Conservation Status:** Critically endangered due to habitat loss and illegal pet trade.

PELICAN

- **Habitat:** Various species found in different regions worldwide.
- **Lifespan:** Around 10-25 years.
- **Diet:** Carnivore; scoop fish into their expandable throat pouches.
- **Behavior:** Large water birds known for their long bills and throat pouches.
- **Conservation Status:** Generally not threatened; adaptable to various habitats.

PENGUIN

- **Habitat:** Various species found in Antarctica and various other regions.
- **Lifespan:** Ranges from 15–20 years, depending on species.
- **Diet:** Carnivore; primarily feeds on fish and krill.
- **Behavior:** Flightless marine birds adapted to aquatic life.
- **Conservation Status:** Some species are threatened due to climate change and fishing activities.

PLATYPUS

● **Habitat:** Found in Australia.

● **Lifespan:** Around 15 years in the wild.

● **Diet:** Carnivore; feeds on insects, larvae, and small vertebrates.

● **Behavior:** Egg-laying mammals with unique features like a duck-like bill.

● **Conservation Status:** Near-threatened due to habitat loss and pollution.

PUMA

- **Habitat:** Found in Argentina.
- **Lifespan:** Typically 8–13 years in the wild.
- **Diet:** Carnivore; hunts various prey animals.
- **Behavior:** Also known as mountain lions or cougars; solitary and territorial.
- **Conservation Status:** Not threatened; adaptable to various habitats.

POLAR BEAR

● **Habitat:** Found in Canada and other Arctic regions.
● **Lifespan:** Around 20-30 years.
● **Diet:** Carnivore; primarily feeds on seals and fish.
● **Behavior:** Largest land carnivores, highly dependent on sea ice for hunting.
● **Conservation Status:** Vulnerable due to climate change impacting their Arctic habitat.

PORCUPINE

- **Habitat:** Found in various regions worldwide.
- **Lifespan:** Typically 5–7 years in the wild.
- **Diet:** Herbivore; feeds on leaves, twigs, and bark.
- **Behavior:** Quilled rodents known for their defensive spines.
- **Conservation Status:** Generally not threatened; adaptable to different habitats.

PANTHER

● **Habitat:** Found in various regions.

● **Lifespan:** Typically 10–12 years in the wild.

● **Diet:** Carnivore; hunts various mammals.

● **Behavior:** Melanistic leopards or jaguars, with dark-colored coats.

● **Conservation Status:** Not a separate species; typically refers to melanistic variants of leopards or jaguars.

PARROT

● **Habitat:** Various species found in different regions worldwide.

● **Lifespan:** Varies among species, generally 20–80 years.

● **Diet:** Omnivore; feeds on fruits, nuts, seeds, and occasionally insects.

● **Behavior:** Intelligent birds known for mimicking human speech and vibrant plumage.

● **Conservation Status:** Some species are threatened due to habitat loss and illegal trade.

PUFFIN

● **Habitat:** Various species found in different regions worldwide.

● **Lifespan:** Around 20 years.

● **Diet:** Carnivore; feeds mainly on fish.

● **Behavior:** Sea birds known for their colorful beaks.

● **Conservation Status:** Some species face threats due to habitat degradation and fishing activities.

QUAIL

- **Habitat:** Woodlands, grasslands, agriculture areas globally.
- **Lifespan:** Typically 2–3 years.
- **Diet:** Omnivore, seeds, insects, vegetation.
- **Behavior:** Ground-dwelling birds forming protective groups.
- **Conservation Status:** Generally stable, facing localized threats.

QUOKKA

- Habitat: Australian scrublands, forests.
- Lifespan: About 10 years.
- Diet: Herbivore, grasses, leaves.
- Behavior: Friendly marsupials with a smiling appearance.
- Conservation Status: Vulnerable due to habitat destruction.

QUOLL

- **Habitat:** Australian forests, grasslands.
- **Lifespan:** 2-5 years in the wild.
- **Diet:** Carnivore, hunting small mammals, reptiles.
- **Behavior:** Nocturnal, solitary marsupials, skilled climbers.
- **Conservation Status:** Endangered due to habitat loss.

QUETZEL

● **Habitat:** Found in Mexico.

● **Lifespan:** Around 20 years in the wild.

● **Diet:** Omnivore; feeds on fruits, insects, and small amphibians.

● **Behavior:** Vibrant-colored birds known for their long tail feathers.

● **Conservation Status:** Near-threatened due to habitat loss.

RACCOON

● **Habitat:** Found in the United States.

● **Lifespan:** Typically 2–3 years in the wild.

● **Diet:** Omnivore; feeds on fruits, nuts, insects, and small animals.

● **Behavior:** Nocturnal mammals with distinctive facial markings.

● **Conservation Status:** Generally not threatened; adaptable to various environments.

RED FOX

● **Habitat:** Found in the United Kingdom.

● **Lifespan:** Typically 2-4 years in the wild.

● **Diet:** Omnivore; feeds on small mammals, birds, fruits, and insects.

● **Behavior:** Agile and intelligent mammals known for their adaptability.

● **Conservation Status:** Generally not threatened; widespread and adaptable.

RED PANDA

● **Habitat:** Found in China.

● **Lifespan:** Around 8-12 years in the wild.

● **Diet:** Primarily herbivores; feed on bamboo, fruits, and insects.

● **Behavior:** Arboreal mammals resembling raccoons, known for their reddish fur and bushy tails.

● **Conservation Status:** Endangered due to habitat loss and illegal trade.

RABBITFISH

● **Habitat:** Found in various oceans.

● **Lifespan:** Typically 5–10 years.

● **Diet:** Herbivore; feeds on algae, plankton, and small invertebrates.

● **Behavior:** Generally peaceful fish often found in coral reefs.

● **Conservation Status:** Not evaluated; some populations may face overfishing threats.

SAIGA ANTELOPE

- **Habitat:** Found in Russia.
- **Lifespan:** Typically 6-10 years.
- **Diet:** Herbivore; feeds on vegetation and grasses.
- **Behavior:** Distinctive antelopes with large noses adapted for filtering dust and cooling air.
- **Conservation Status:** Critically endangered due to poaching and habitat loss.

SEA LION

● **Habitat:** Found in various coastal regions.

● **Lifespan:** Around 20-30 years.

● **Diet:** Carnivore; feeds on fish and squid.

● **Behavior:** Pinnipeds known for their agility in water.

● **Conservation Status:** Some populations are threatened due to fishing and habitat degradation.

SNOW LEOPARD

- **Habitat:** Found in China.
- **Lifespan:** Around 15–18 years in the wild.
- **Diet:** Carnivore; hunts mountain goats, sheep, and other small mammals.
- **Behavior:** Elusive big cats adapted to cold, rugged terrain.
- **Conservation Status:** Endangered due to poaching and habitat fragmentation.

SLOTH

- Habitat: Found in Brazil.
- Lifespan: Around 20-30 years in the wild.
- Diet: Herbivore; primarily feeds on leaves and buds.
- Behavior: Slow-moving mammals spending most of their time in trees.
- Conservation Status: Generally not threatened; habitat loss affects some populations.

TORTOISE

● **Habitat:** Various species found in different regions worldwide.

● **Lifespan:** Varies among species; can exceed 100 years.

● **Diet:** Herbivore; primarily feeds on grasses, leaves, and fruits.

● **Behavior:** Slow-moving reptiles with protective shells.

● **Conservation Status:** Some species are endangered due to habitat loss and illegal trade.

TOUCAN

- **Habitat:** Found in Brazil.
- **Lifespan:** Typically 15–20 years in the wild.
- **Diet:** Omnivore; feeds on fruits, insects, and small reptiles.
- **Behavior:** Birds known for their large, colorful bills.
- **Conservation Status:** Generally not threatened; widespread in suitable habitats.

TERN

● Habitat: Various species found in different regions worldwide.

● Lifespan: Typically around 10 years.

● Diet: Carnivore; feeds on fish and insects.

● Behavior: Agile seabirds known for their graceful flight.

● Conservation Status: Some populations face threats due to habitat loss and disturbances.

U, V, W

URCHIN

- **Habitat:** Various species found in oceans worldwide.
- **Lifespan:** Varies by species; some can live for several years.
- **Diet:** Herbivore; grazes on algae and organic debris.
- **Behavior:** Small marine invertebrates with spiny shells.
- **Conservation Status:** Not evaluated; important for maintaining marine ecosystem balance.

VULTURE

- **Habitat:** Various species found in different regions worldwide.
- **Lifespan:** Around 20–30 years.
- **Diet:** Scavenger; feeds on carrion and dead animals.
- **Behavior:** Large birds with excellent soaring abilities and keen eyesight.
- **Conservation Status:** Some species are threatened due to habitat loss and poisoning.

VICUNAS

- **Habitat:** Found in Argentina.
- **Lifespan:** Around 15-20 years.
- **Diet:** Herbivore; grazes on grasses and plants.
- **Behavior:** Wild relatives of alpacas and llamas known for their fine wool.
- **Conservation Status:** Near-threatened due to poaching for their valuable wool.

WALRUS

- Habitat: Arctic regions.
- Lifespan: Around 40 years.
- Diet: Carnivore; primarily feeds on clams, mollusks, and small invertebrates.
- Behavior: Large pinnipeds known for their tusks and social structures.
- Conservation Status: Vulnerable due to climate change affecting their Arctic habitat.

WILDEBEEST

● **Habitat:** Found in Kenya.

● **Lifespan:** Around 20 years in the wild.

● **Diet:** Herbivore; graze on grasses and plants.

● **Behavior:** Large antelopes known for their migratory herds and mass movements.

● **Conservation Status:** Not threatened; populations occur in significant numbers.

WRASSE

- **Habitat:** Found in tropical and subtropical waters.
- **Lifespan:** Varies among species; some can live for over 30 years.
- **Diet:** Carnivore; feeds on small invertebrates and parasites
- **Behavior:** Colorful fish often found near coral reefs.
- **Conservation Status:** Not evaluated; some species are sought after in the aquarium trade.

XENOPUS

- **Habitat:** Found in various countries in Africa.
- **Lifespan:** Typically around 5–15 years.
- **Diet:** Carnivore; feeds on insects, small fish, and crustaceans.
- **Behavior:** Aquatic frogs with webbed feet and distinctively clawed toes.
- **Conservation Status:** Not evaluated; widely used in scientific research and as pets

XIPHIAS (SWORDFISH)

- ● Habitat: Found in various oceans.
- ● Lifespan: Around 9-12 years.
- ● Diet: Carnivore; preys on smaller fish and cephalopods.
- ● Behavior: Large predatory fish known for their elongated bill-like snouts.
- ● Conservation Status: Not threatened; however, subject to overfishing in some regions.

YELLOWTAIL

- **Habitat:** Found in various oceans.
- **Lifespan:** Varies by species; typically around 10-12 years.
- **Diet:** Carnivore; feeds on smaller fish and squid.
- **Behavior:** Fast-swimming fish known for their yellow tails.
- **Conservation Status:** Some species are targeted for commercial fishing.

YAK

- Habitat: Found in Himalayan regions.
- Lifespan: Around 20 years.
- Diet: Herbivore; grazes on grasses and plants at high altitudes.
- Behavior: Domesticated bovids adapted to harsh mountainous environments.
- Conservation Status: Not threatened; important livestock for local communities.

ZEBRA

● **Habitat:** Various species found in Africa.

● **Lifespan:** Typically around 20–30 years in the wild.

● **Diet:** Herbivore; graze on grasses and leaves.

● **Behavior:** Striped equids known for their social structures and herd behaviors.

● **Conservation Status:** Not threatened; populations occur in significant numbers.

ZANDER

● **Habitat:** Found in freshwater habitats in Europe.

● **Lifespan:** Around 10-15 years.

● **Diet:** Carnivore; feeds on smaller fish and invertebrates.

● **Behavior:** Predatory fish with a preference for still or slow-flowing waters.

● **Conservation Status:** Not evaluated; popular among anglers.

ZOSTERA (EELGRASS)

- Habitat: Found in marine coastal habitats.
- Lifespan: Varies based on environmental conditions.
- Role: Important marine plant providing habitats and food for various marine species.
- Behavior: Forms extensive underwater meadows crucial for marine biodiversity.
- Conservation Status: Sensitive to pollution and coastal development; efforts made for conservation.

ZEBU

- **Habitat:** Various regions.
- **Lifespan:** Around 15–20 years.
- **Diet:** Herbivore; graze on grasses and leaves.
- **Behavior:** Domesticated cattle adapted to warm climates.
- **Conservation Status:** Not threatened; valuable livestock in various cultures.

Acknowledgment

I thank God who inspires me to write. Thanks to my lovely wife. Also thanks to my amazing children and students to whom I have told stories, for many years. I also thank my dear friend Abhinav Gupta for the tremendous illustrations. Also, thanks to my brilliant proofreaders. – James Benedict

Author

James Benedict Is a teacher, writer, and storyteller. He is the founder of Emmanuel Literacy Foundation. James is also the author of Unlikely Friends, The Bully's Foe, The Move, The Contest, Success Disguised, and The Mystery Box and is working on many more books. His stories show goodness can come in hopeless situations. James travels, teaches, and inspires people of all ages. He has taught in top Universities in Taiwan and Japan.

NOTE

As we witness the diversity and fragility of these creatures, let's remember the importance of preserving and respecting the natural world. Their stories remind us of our responsibility to protect these species and their habitats, ensuring a harmonious coexistence for generations to come. Join us on this journey to appreciate and safeguard the wonders of the animal kingdom.

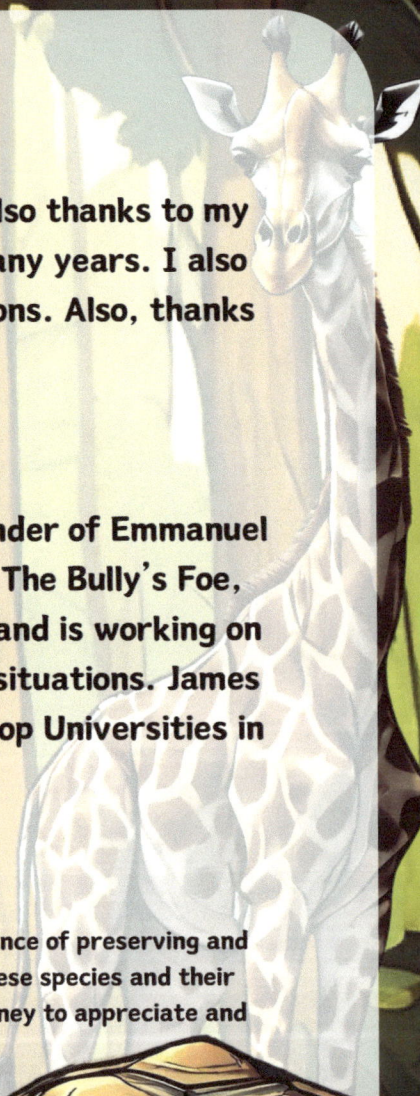

www.ingramcontent.com/pod-product-compliance
Lightning Source LLC
Chambersburg PA
CBHW041112050426

42335CB00045B/180